Mel Bay Presents

# Light so Brilliant

## Christmas Carols and Tunes for Solo Harp

By Stephanie Claussen

The arrangements in this book are intended for intermediate to advanced lever or pedal harpists. The lowest note is C two octaves below middle C; the hightest note is G two and a half octaves above middle C.

www.melbay.com

# About the Author

Twin Cities harpist Stephanie Claussen spent a year fulfilling one of her dreams: arranging and refining twenty-one of her favorite carols and tunes, most of which are French. She crafted original interludes and countermelodies aiming to season familiar tunes with just enough spice to keep audiences surprised while steering clear of modern harmonies. Claussen's companion recording, *Light so Brilliant: Carols and Tunes for Christmas,* is available on her website, iTunes, Amazon, and CD Baby.

Claussen started harp at the age of seven, playing on a Musicmakers Gothic lever harp that her father built. She later obtained her Bachelors of Music at the University of Minnesota and she now teaches and performs full-time in her hometown of St. Paul, Minnesota. She has released four solo albums and has been involved in various collaborative recording projects. Her performance venues range from the concert hall stage to coffee shops and the lanes of the Minnesota Renaissance Festival.

For information on performances and recordings by Stephanie Claussen, visit: www.StephanieClaussen.com.

# Contents

# The Holly and the Ivy/Masters in the Hall

Arranged by Stephanie Claussen

Traditional English/Traditional French

* All harmonics are optional; notes may be played where written.

Gm
D
Gm
D
Gm
Cm
E♭
Gm
D
Gm
pp
Cm
E♭
D
Gm
f
F♮
Cm
Gm
Cm
Gm
mp
f
mp
F♯
Cm
Gm
Dm
E♭
Gm
Cm
mp
cresc.
F♮
F♯
Gm
Dm
Gm
F♮
B♮
E♮ F♯
molto rit.

*Tempo primo*

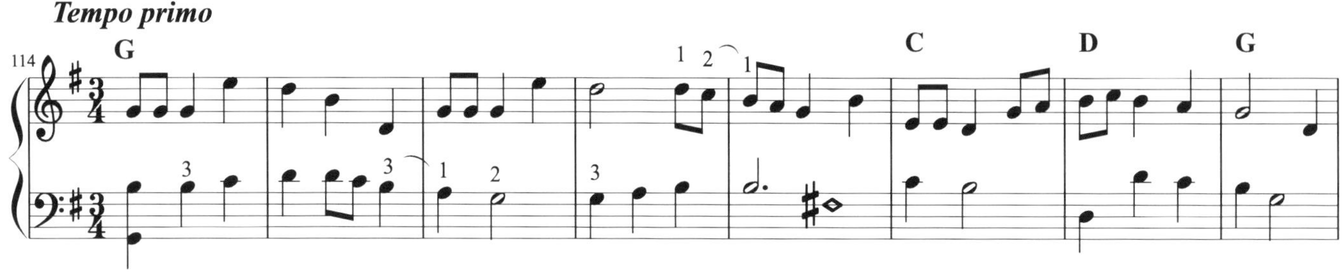

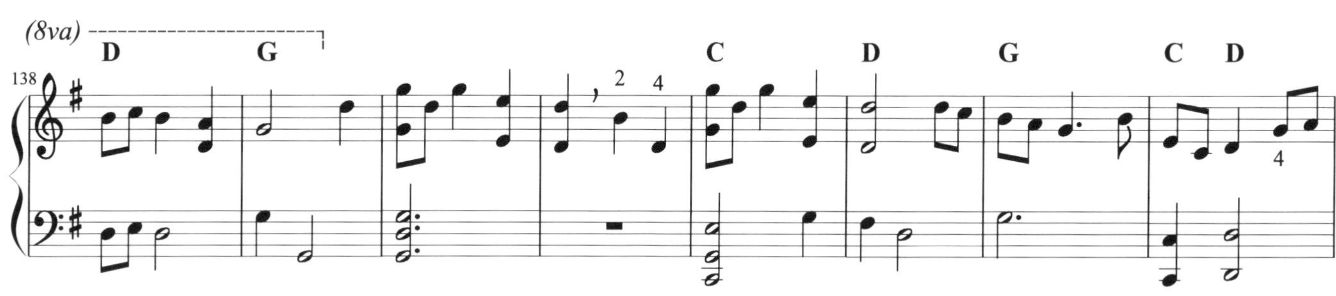

3.15"

# We Three Kings of Orient Are

Arranged by Stephanie Claussen

by John Henry Hopkins

D
G
Am
C
Am
Em
RH
D
Em
D
Em
D
G
Bm
Am
C
Em
D
Em
C
D
Em
C
D
Em
D
Am
D
E
G
C
Em

127
Em

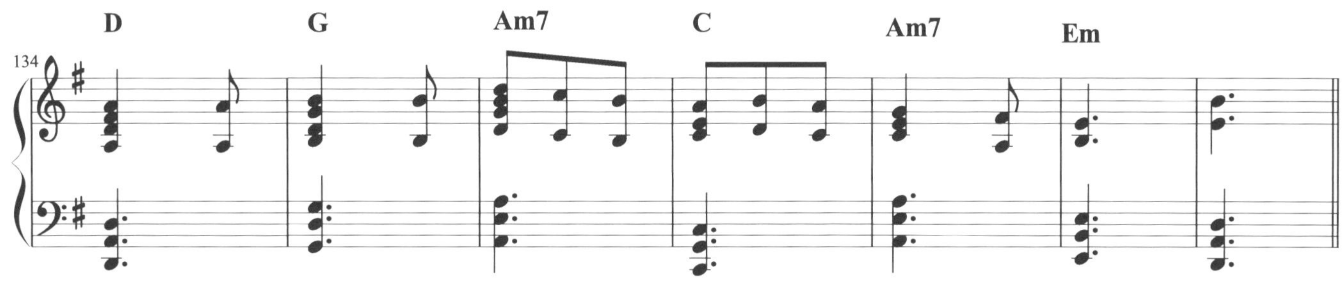
134
D
G
Am7
C
Am7
Em

Mysteriously
141

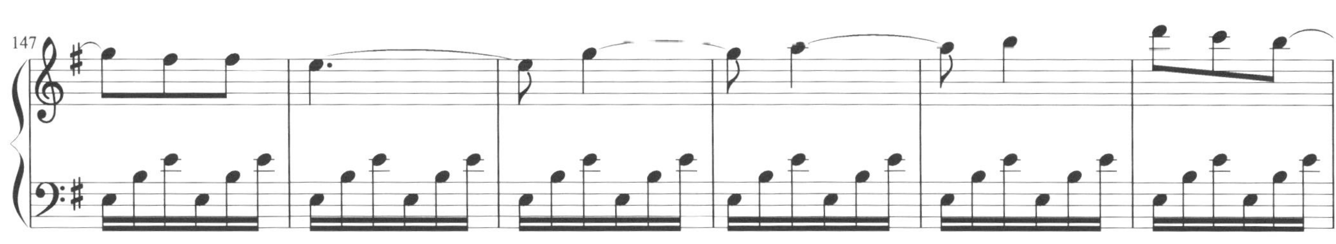
147

153
fade
3.30"

# Noël Nouvelet

Arranged by Stephanie Claussen

Traditional French

8va Right Hand
Am G C G Am Em G Am G Am
mf
(8va)
G Am Em Am Em Am G Am
(8va)
G Am G Am G Am
G Am G Am G Am Em
mp
Am Em Am G Em Am G Am
1.
G Am
2.
G Am
fade

3.09"

# Bring a Torch, Jeannette, Isabella

Arranged by Stephanie Claussen

Traditional French

66
G Am D G Em D G
gliss.
75
D C G D Em D G
85
D Em G D Em D G G
96
C D G Em G D G Em
105
C D G D C G D
113
Em Em7 C G Am G Em

120
D G D Em C D G D G
131
C
140
D G Em G D G Am D
mp
149
G Em D G C
gliss.
158
G D Em D G D Em G
167
D Em D G

3.37"

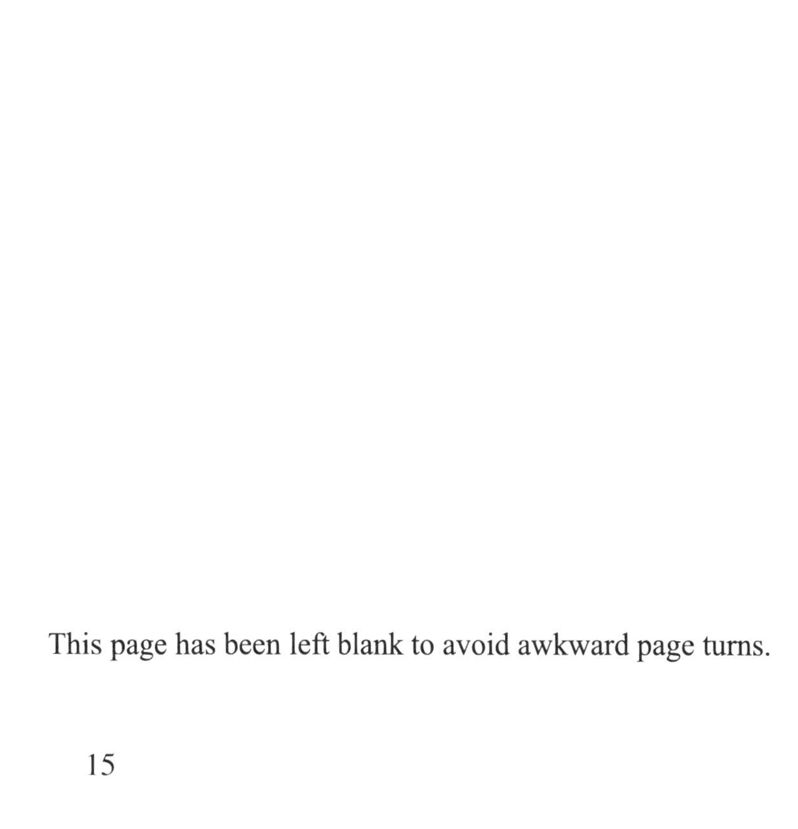

This page has been left blank to avoid awkward page turns.

# Willie Take Your Little Drum/Il Est Né, Le Divin Enfant

Arranged by Stephanie Claussen

Traditional French

**Solemnly**

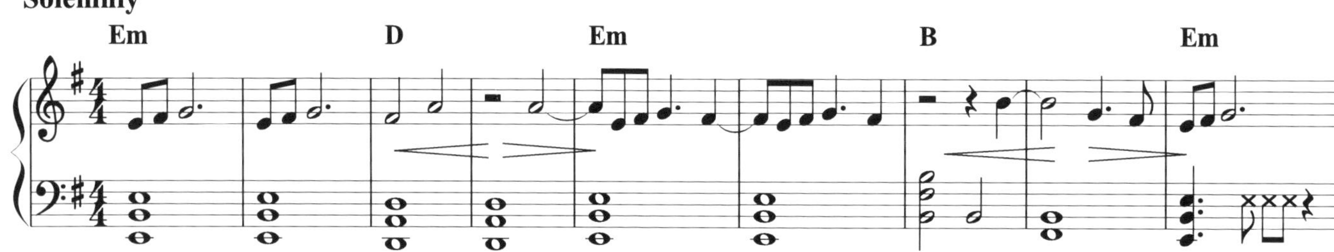


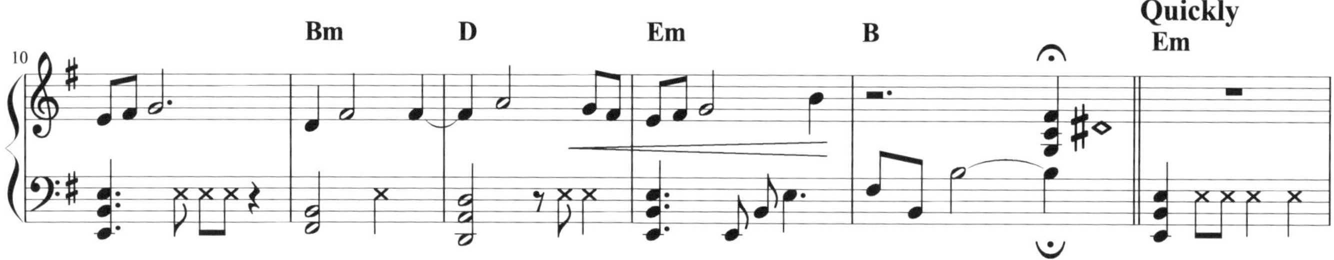

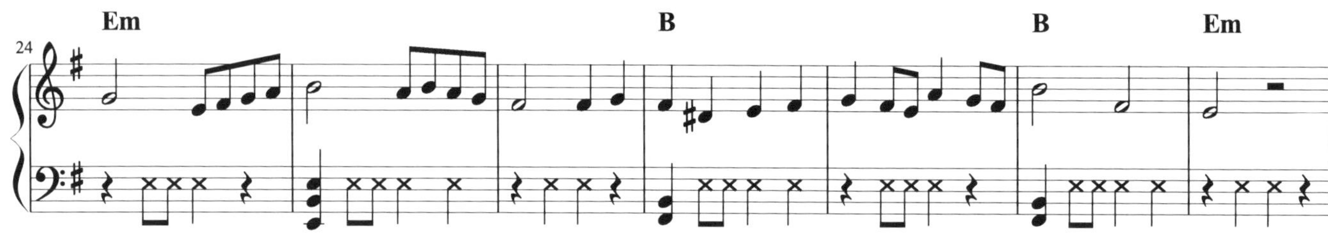

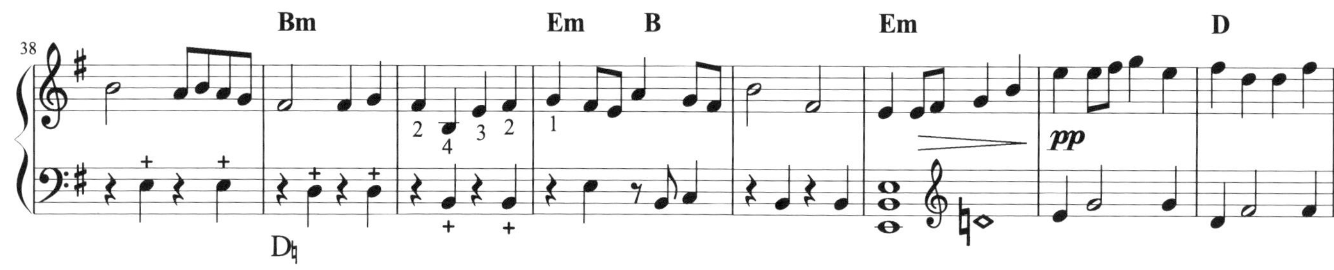

Em Bm Em D Em Bm Em
mf
f subito pp
D Em D B Em Am B D
mp
D♯ D♮ D♯
Em Em D Em
mf pp
D♮
Bm Em B Em B
mf
D♯
Em D Em Bm Em
p mf
D♮
B Em D Em G
f
D♯ D♮

88
G C D G Em C G D
4
4
ff

97
G D G C D G C D G
4
4
mp

105
G9 G G9 G

112
C D G Am D

119
G C D G Am D G G9
3

126
G C G

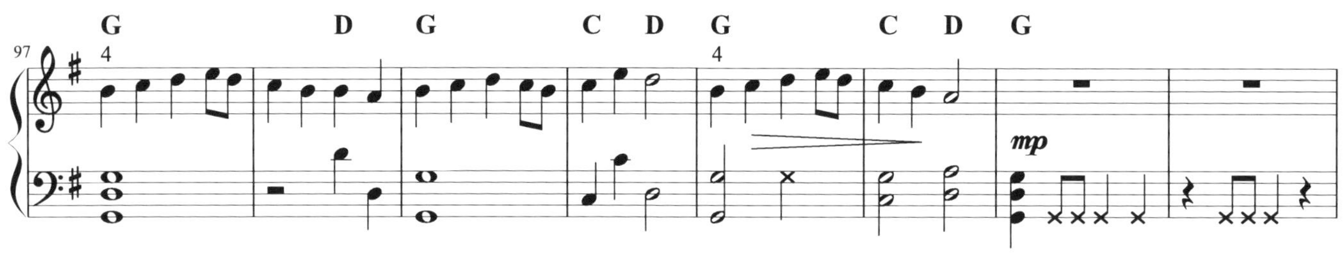

3.15"

This page has been left blank to avoid awkward page turns.

# Shepherds, Shake Off Your Drowsy Slumber

Arranged by Stephanie Claussen

Traditional French

*The melody is in the LH.
4 (2nd time)
rit.
8va Right Hand
gliss.
(8va)
Lento
cresc.
*Bring out the E♭ drone.
3.29"

# Let All Mortal Flesh Keep Silence

Arranged by Stephanie Claussen

Traditional French

*Pedal harpists may include a D♯ as desired in both RH and LH.

3.00"

# 'Twas in the Moon of Wintertime/Ding Dong Merrily On High

Arranged by Stephanie Claussen

Traditional French

68
F C F C G Am
77
Em F G C
8va Both Hands
F G C G Am F
85
(8va)
G Em F G C G C G C
mf
mp
97
G F C Dm C G Am C
mf
106
F G C
8va Both Hands
G F G
112
(8va)
Am Em F G C Am G Am C
p

121
Em Am Em Am G Am
129
G F Em Dm G C G F C Am
p
mf
138
Em F G C C G C G
145
Am Em F G C C Dm C
f
Tempo primo
152
G Am Em F G C Am
159

167
Dm
Am
Em
Am

8va Right Hand
175
Am
Em
Am
Fm

(8va)
184
Am
Em
Am
G
Am

(8va)
192
D
Em
Am
G
Am
G

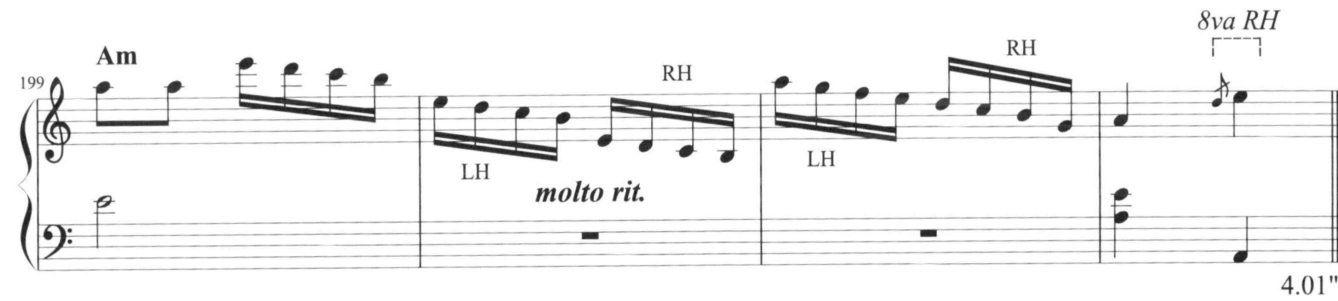
199
Am
LH
RH
molto rit.
LH
RH
8va RH
4.01"

# The Snow Lay On the Ground/A Rose by My Early Morning Walk

Arranged by Stephanie Claussen

Traditional Irish/English

31
E
G♯m
B7
E
A
p

37
A
D
E

43
A
mf
Bm
F♯m
Bm

50
E
A
E
A
B7
E
f
D♯

54
A
E
F♯m
B
E
mp

58
E
A
B
E
C♯m
4 4

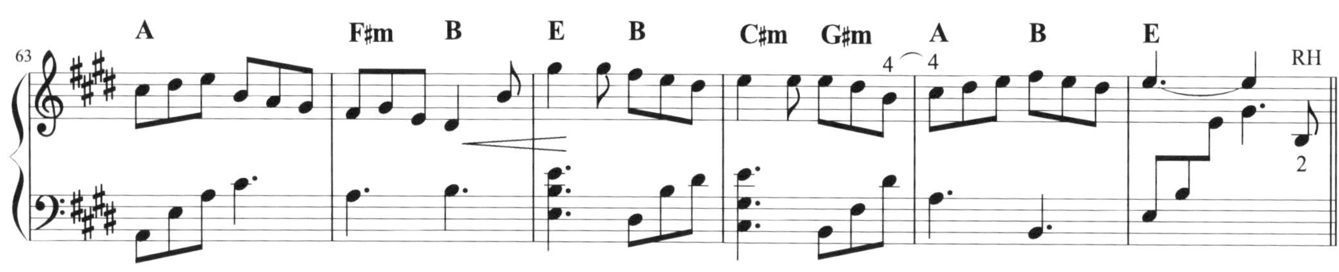
63
A
F♯m
B
E
B
C♯m
G♯m
A
B
E
RH
4 4
2

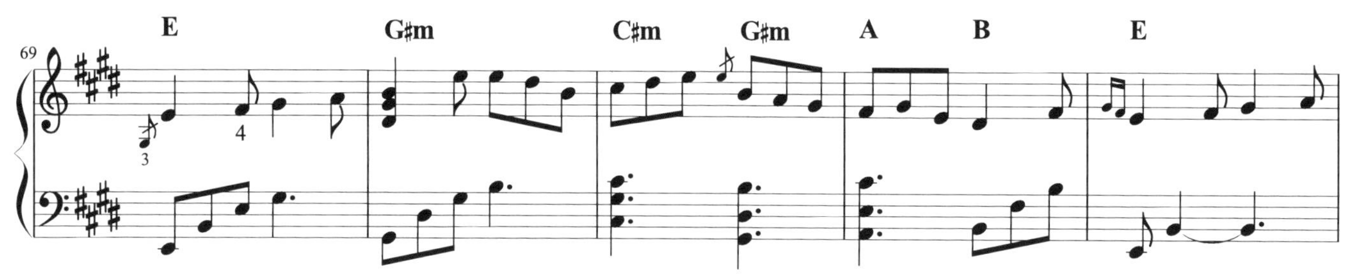
69
E
G♯m
C♯m
G♯m
A
B
E
3
4

74
G♯m
A
F♯m
E
C♯m
4 4
4

79
A
F♯m
B
E
B
C♯m
E
A
B
4 4

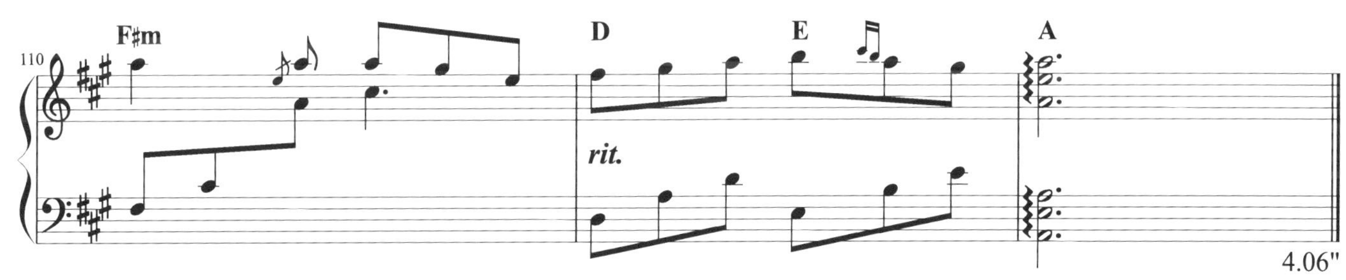


4.06"

# The Traveler Benighted in Snow/The Bonfire

Arranged by Stephanie Claussen

Traditional Scottish

*Save some ornaments for the repeat.

Dm
F
Am
C
F
Dm
f

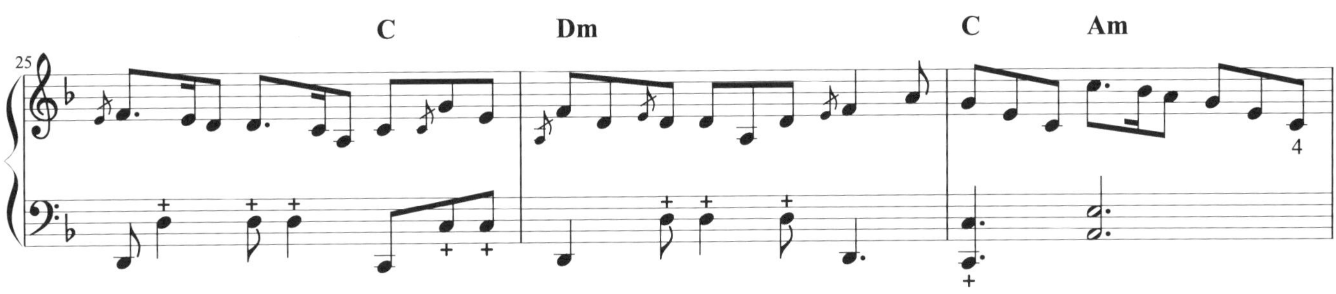
C
Dm
C
Am

F
Am7
Dm
p
C
Dm
B♭

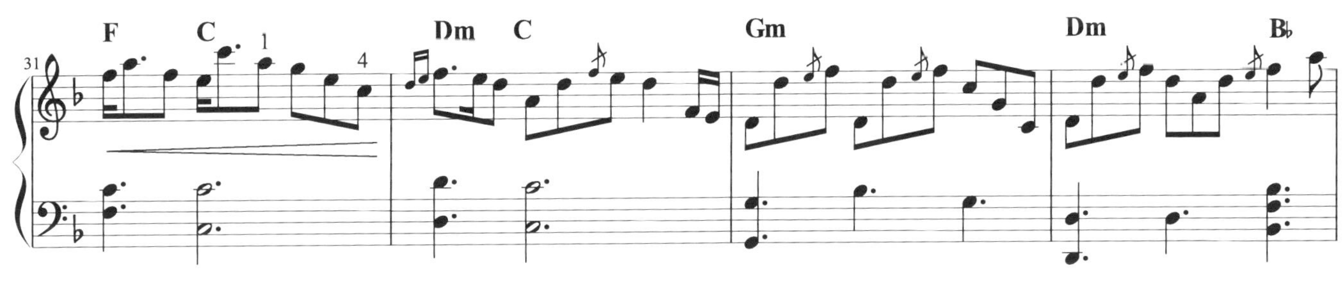
F
C
Dm
C
Gm
Dm
B♭

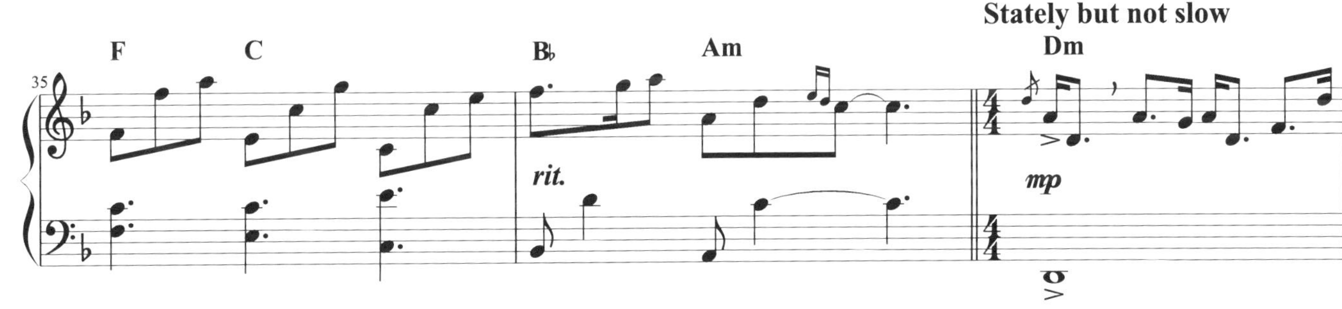
F
C
B♭
Am
rit.
Stately but not slow
Dm
mp

38
C
Dm
Am
Dm
mf
42
C
Dm
Am
Dm
f
46
C
Dm
Am
Dm
C
pp
50
Am
Dm
Am
Dm
C
Dm
cresc.
ff
54
C
Dm
Am
Dm
58
Am
Dm
C
Dm

62
C
Dm
Cm B♭
Dm C
pp
66
F C
Dm
Am Dm
8va Right Hand
mf
(8va)
70
B♭ C
Dm
B♭ C Dm
74
C
Dm
Am Dm C
78
C
Dm
F Am Dm
Am
82
F C
Dm
Am Dm
5.21"

# Green Groweth the Holly/God Rest Ye Merry Gentlemen

Arranged by Stephanie Claussen

16th century English

*Pedal harpists may jump up an octave in the RH.

# Bourrée d'Avignon or Parson's Farewell

Arranged by Stephanie Claussen

Traditional French

47
Dm
Am
F
C
54
Dm
Am
Dm
F
C
61
Dm
Am
Dm
C
Dm
Am
p
69
Dm
C
Dm
Am
F
mf
f
76
C
Dm
Am
Dm
F
83
C
Dm
Am
Dm
molto rit.
2.40"

# O Come O Come Emmanuel

Arranged by Stephanie Claussen

Traditional French

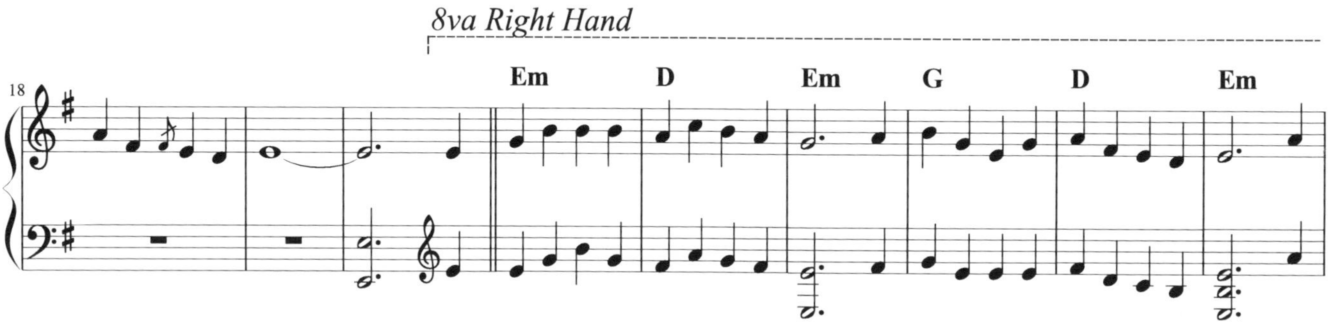

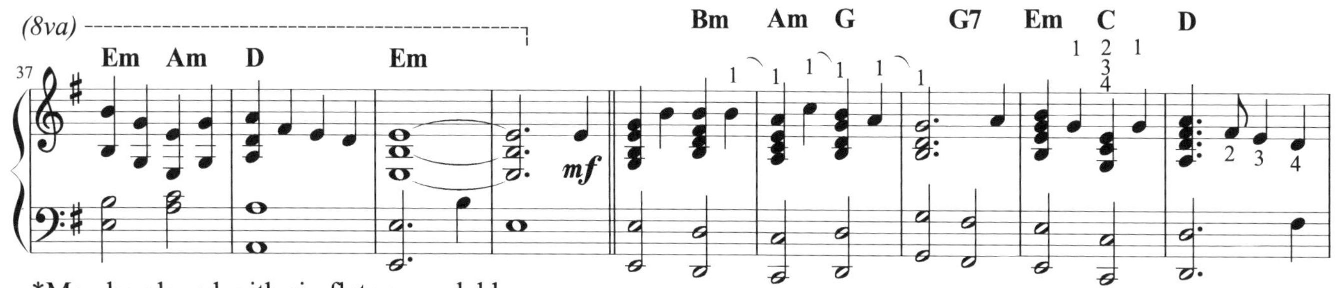


*May be played with six flats on pedal harp

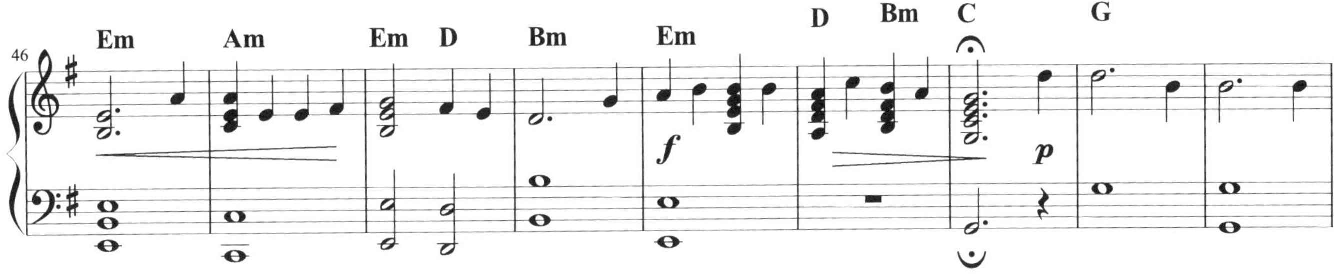
46
Em Am Em D Bm Em D Bm C G
f
p

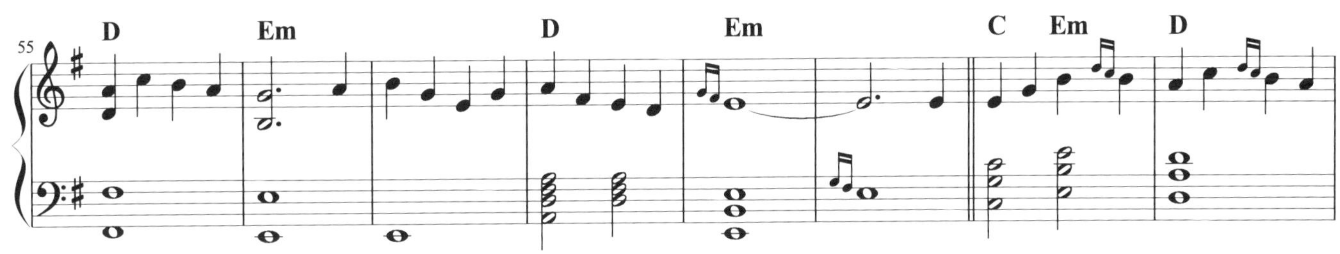
55
D Em D Em C Em D

63
Em C Am Bm Em D C Em Bm

70
Em Am G Em D Em G Em

8va Both Hands
78
Am D Em Em Am D Em
3.30"

# Ce Jour de L'An

Arranged by Stephanie Claussen

Pedal harp version

by Guillaume Dufay

𝅗𝅥=104

*Fine*

D.C. al Fine
pp
C♮
B♮
C♯
B♭
2.51"

# Ce Jour de l'An

Arranged by Stephanie Claussen

Lever harp version

by Guillaume Dufay

Set Middle C♯ and B♭ above Middle C

mp
mf
pp
D.C. al Fine
2.15"

# Whence Is That Goodly Fragrance Flowing?

Arranged by Stephanie Claussen

Traditional French

*Glisses can be played with either 2 or 3, ending on 1.

*Bring out the melody.

1.
2.
Am
G
C
Am
F
Am
G
C
53
4
4
61
mf
F
C
71
G
C
Am
F
G
C
G
legato
81
Am
C
F
C
G
Am
F
Am
91
G
C
F
p
1 4
100
C
Am
G
C
8va Right Hand
rit.
p
pp
3.50"

# Recordings Featuring Stephanie Claussen

*Renaissance and Celtic Harp*
by Stephanie Claussen

*Rose - Celtic Harp*
by Stephanie Claussen
"Fourteen delightful melodies from the British Isles"

*Lord of Love*
by Acoustic Nerve
"Original music by John Shank with guitar, harp, fiddle and vocals"

*Soirée à Montpellier*
by Stephanie Claussen
"Musical snapshots of Southern France"

*Glory of God*
by Hearts and Harps
"A meaningful musical journey through God's Word"

*Light so Brilliant: Carols and Tunes for Christmas*
by Stephanie Claussen
"A harp album of medieval Christmas splendor"

*Faireborne*
by the Ravenscroft Musicke Guild
"Old tunes for new ears"

For sound clips and information on purchasing these recordings, visit:
www.StephanieClaussen.com.